Guidelines for
Multilingual Deaf Education
Teacher Preparation Programs

Multilingual Deaf Education
Teacher Training, Research, and Pedagogy

Volume 1   *Guidelines for Multilingual Deaf Education Teacher Preparation Programs*

Guidelines for Multilingual Deaf Education Teacher Preparation Programs

Christopher Kurz, Debbie Golos, Marlon Kuntze, Jonathan Henner, and Jessica Scott

Gallaudet University Press
in partnership with the
American College Educators of the Deaf and Hard of Hearing
Multilingual Education Special Interest Group

Gallaudet University Press
gupress.gallaudet.edu

Gallaudet University Press is located on the
traditional territories of Nacotchtank and Piscataway.

ISBN 978-1-944838-95-9 (paperback)
ISBN 978-1-944838-96-6 (ebook)
ISBN 978-1-944838-97-3 (Manifold)

Cover art by Mia Sanchez. *Diversity of Light and Love*. Acrylic on canvas.

Cover description: In the center of the cover is an acrylic painting with a prism in the center of the canvas with hands of different skin tones facing each other inside the prism. A spectrum of colors radiates from the prism on the right, and white light on the left. Hands of different skin tones are placed within the spectrum and white light. Above the painting is the title: GUIDELINES FOR MULTILINGUAL DEAF EDUCATION TEACHER PREPARATION PROGRAMS. Below the painting are the author names: Christopher Kurz, Debbie Golos, Marlon Kuntze, Jonathan Henner, and Jessica Scott.

Note From the Authors

As authors of these guidelines, we recognize that we are all white. We want to thank BIPOC members of Deaf communities and of the MLE-SIG for providing their feedback to ensure that we would present a perspective that aligns with a multilingual, multicultural, multimodal perspective and honors home/heritage languages, cultures, race, gender, abilities, and other multiple and intersecting identities. We also wanted to mention that in a previous version of these guidelines, we used the term "BE-SIG" throughout. Our name has since changed to the Multilingual Education Special Interest Group, and "BE-SIG" has been changed to "MLE-SIG" to reflect that.

Additionally, we wanted to recognize the ongoing discussions and perspectives that have changed and are still in the process of changing since we wrote this document. This includes terminology regarding antiracist, antibias education; varying perspectives on social justice, transformative justice, and restorative justice; and terms of identity including Deaf, deaf, Hard of Hearing, DeafDisabled, DeafBlind, LGBTQIA+, etc.

With all this in mind, we feel it is important to also acknowledge our awareness of our own bias and privilege.

We welcome continued and ongoing conversations and invite you to join us on this journey.

Note From the Publisher

To view an open access version of these guidelines, along with video summaries in American Sign Language, please go to https://gallaudetupress.manifoldapp.org and click on the front cover image of these guidelines.

Guidelines for
Multilingual Deaf Education
Teacher Preparation Programs

The following guidelines for Deaf education teacher preparation programs are a product of multiple conversations that took place over several years among the members of the American College Educators of the Deaf and Hard of Hearing (ACEDHH) Multilingual Education Special Interest Group (MLE-SIG). The Deaf[1] and hearing members of the MLE-SIG are instructors and researchers in various bilingual teacher preparation programs across the United States and Canada. These discussions led us to realize there was a need for a series of publications related to "Multilingual Deaf Education" (see definition on p. 12). Additional publications in the series will address topics such as the history of bilingual education and research on Multilingual Deaf Education. Particularly given the current political and social climate, we agreed that, as a priority, the first publication in the series should include guidelines for teacher preparation programs.

The goal of the guidelines is to support the effort to create transformative curricular changes within teacher preparation programs by providing guidance for how to transition to or align with a Multilingual Deaf Education perspective. Programs that apply a multilingual lens to Deaf education are in a better position to produce teachers who are knowledgeable about the diverse language needs of Deaf students. We also recognize that Deaf education teacher preparation programs need to provide training related to issues of language deprivation (see Hall et al., 2019), in addition to advocating for and implementing pedagogy that is antibias, antiracist, antiableist, and queer friendly (see Derman-Sparks et al., 2020).

With the current shortage of teachers of the Deaf and the number leaving schools in the near future, approximately 500 new teachers will be needed in the next few years (CEASD, 2020; CEASD-NAD, 2018; Luft, n.d.). The growing shortage makes it a critical time to reexamine teacher preparation

---

1. See pp. 12–16 for terms.

programs in the United States and Canada.[2] This is an opportunity to ensure we are providing high quality education to the next generation of teachers, so that they are more prepared to meet the growing diversity in the Deaf student population and to teach them multilingually and multimodally.

Since the publication of *Unlocking the Curriculum* (Johnson et al., 1989), there have been bilingual education reforms in educational settings serving Deaf students, including the adoption of bilingual pedagogy planning and in-service bilingual education professional development for teachers of the Deaf. The number of bilingual teacher preparation programs is also growing, along with numerous research articles published that explore the positive benefits that sign language has on student growth and development; we will return to this in forthcoming series publications.

Despite insufficient resources or curricula, schools/programs serving Deaf students and teacher preparation programs still strive to understand, define, and apply sign language strategically in academic environments to support language and content learning. Technologies that integrate sign language use in the classroom (e.g., Canvas, FlipGrid, Google Classroom, VoiceThread, Zoom) have become cheaper and more widely available. However, for educators, the task of integrating and implementing sign languages for the full range of educational activities continues to be challenging. The MLE-SIG has identified the following barriers to successfully implementing quality multilingual education:

- Classroom resources, instructional practices, and communication policies continue to be oriented toward the use and development of spoken and written English (Simms & Thumann, 2007).

- The growing awareness of audism in Deaf education, especially from educational professionals, that prohibits Deaf students from advancing in signing environments. For example, schools prioritize auditory services over American Sign Language (ASL) immersion services.

- There has been no clear and current definition of what bilingual Deaf education means.

---

2. While these guidelines will be targeted to teacher preparation programs in the United States and Canada using ASL and English, the contents still apply and can be modified as international programs see fit.

- There has been a lack of consistency within and across educational settings that adopt a bilingual philosophy.

- There has been a lack of consistency across Deaf education teacher preparation programs on key competencies, such as sign language proficiency, comparative linguistics of ASL and English, and ASL and English bilingual methodologies and strategies.

- There are not enough Deaf and signing-fluent hearing teachers who can serve as fluent language models.

- In Deaf education, the percentages of P–12 teachers who are Black, Indigenous, and people of color (BIPOC) do not reflect the number of students with diverse linguistic and cultural backgrounds (Simms et al., 2008).

- The percentages of faculty and instructors in teacher training programs who are BIPOC do not reflect the number of students with diverse linguistic and cultural backgrounds.

- The curricula and teaching approaches are out of step with the current Deaf student population, which has undergone significant change over the past few decades. This is due not only to increased immigration but also to the growing awareness of racial and ethnic diversity that exists in the student population, and the recognition of sexual orientation (i.e., lesbian, gay, bisexual, transgender, queer, asexual, and intersex) and gender diversity among students (e.g., Denninger, 2017).

Our recognition of the aforementioned barriers has contributed to conversations on how we can improve teacher preparation programs.

Again, our goal is to support teacher preparation programs in their efforts to align with a multilingual perspective for Deaf education. An anticipated short-term outcome of the guidelines is an increase in teacher preparation programs that transition to or begin the process of transitioning to a multilingual perspective for Deaf education. We anticipate the following long-term outcomes: (a) an increase in the number of fluent language models for Deaf children in varying educational environments, (b) an increase in the number of high-quality teachers with competencies in multilingual strategies, (c) an increase in the number of diverse high-quality teacher educators in teacher preparation programs, and (d) an increase in collaboration among teacher preparation programs.

In the following sections we will discuss: (1) our theoretical framework, including common terms; (2) key components for high quality multilingual teacher preparation programs; and (3) next steps.

THEORETICAL FRAMEWORK

In preparing the guidelines, we considered multiple theoretical perspectives that take into account language, current perspectives and pedagogy in Deaf education, and antiaudist, antibias, antiracist education. This includes the tenets from Critical Race Theory (centrality of racism in daily life; white supremacy; narratives and storytelling; interest convergence and intersectionality; see Crenshaw et al., 1995) and how they have been adapted to account for Deaf perspectives (centrality of audism; linguistic oppression; hearing supremacy; sharing narratives and coping strategies; interest convergence; and intersectionality; see Rosen, 2017), while also aligning with current effective practices and antibias and antiracist education (four goals: identity, diversity, justice and activism; see Derman-Sparks et al., 2020). Further, we use a framework for early literacy (Kuntze & Golos, 2021; see Figure 1) that aligns with the whole child approach (Slade & Griffith, 2013), along with what we currently know about the impacts of language deprivation (Hall et al., 2017).

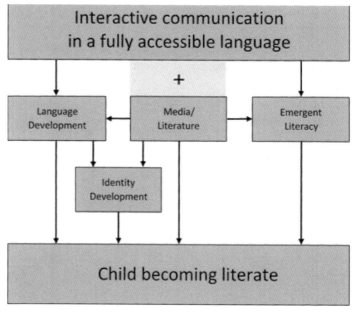

Figure 1. *Framework for early literacy (Kuntze & Golos, 2021).*

Finally, we align with two of the five propositions in the Deaf pedagogy framework recently proposed by Skyer (2020): the adapted tools proposition and the multimodal proposition. While it is beyond the scope of this paper to go into detail about each of these theoretical perspectives, in combination they led us to develop a framework for Multilingual Deaf Education teacher preparation (see Figure 2). We use this framework as a foundation for our recommendations for key components in a Multilingual Deaf Education teacher preparation program.

REDEFINING BILINGUAL-BICULTURAL IN THE 21ST CENTURY

Our conversations across multiple years led us to develop these guidelines with the aim to redefine what bilingual Deaf education means in the 21st century. We recognize that the definition of bilingual Deaf education previously included the word "bicultural" as well (i.e., bilingual-bicultural). However, it is now recognized that culture is already embedded within the term "bilingual," meaning that all cultures, including Deaf culture, are naturally part of bilingual education.

In considering today's climate of multilingual learners and that culture is now recognized as a key component of multilingual education, we have chosen to use the term "Multilingual Deaf Education." Some common terms related to Multilingual Deaf Education that we will use throughout the paper are as follows:

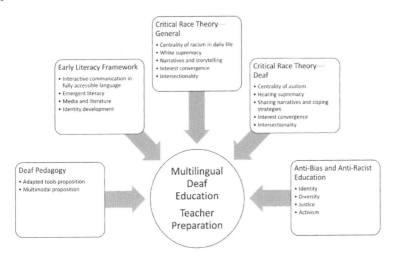

Figure 2. *Multilingual Deaf Education Teacher Preparation Theoretical Framework (Kuntze & Golos, 2021).*

Deaf. We define the term "Deaf" to include all Deaf and hard of hearing people who use ASL (or other sign languages) and English (or other languages), including DeafBlind (Larsen & Damen, 2014), DeafDisabled (Burke, 2014), and late-deafened people, regardless of varying hearing levels, signing levels, cultures, identities, and home language usage.

Multilingual Deaf Education. We define "Multilingual Deaf Education" as the practice of using two or more languages for the teaching of academic content (Valdés et al., 2015), one of which is the sign language of the Deaf community. Increasingly, we see Deaf students from homes representing multiple ethnic and racial cultures (e.g., Black, Latinx, Indigenous, immigrant) and multiple spoken and signed languages (Cannon et al., 2016; Gallaudet Research Institute, 2013; Gárate-Estes et al., in press; Musyoka & Adeoye, 2020). We also recognize intersectionality and the multiple identities and abilities of Deaf students (Dunn & Anderson, 2019; Gárate-Estes et al., in press; García-Fernández, 2020; Leigh et al., 2020; Pichler et al., 2019). It is critical to consider these factors when redefining what Multilingual Deaf Education means in the 21st century.

In the United States and parts of Canada, Deaf students in Multilingual Deaf Education settings use both ASL and English as the primary languages of curriculum, instruction, and assessment.[3] Multilingual schools that serve Deaf children from homes using languages other than ASL and English (e.g., Deaf children from families who use Spanish, Lengua de Señas Mexicana [LSM], Navajo, Somali, or Arabic) should honor students' use of their home languages (Musyoka & Adeoye, 2020). Deaf education teacher preparation programs should support their teacher candidates' language fluency development, plus provide techniques and tools to tap the diverse languages, cultures, resources, and creativity of Deaf communities and Deaf students, in order to support learning in the classroom.

Multiculturalism. "Multiculturalism" is defined as the acknowledgement and respect of two or more cultures within the educational curriculum, one of which is Deaf culture (Leigh et al., 2020). This

---

3. Deaf students in the other parts of Canada use Quebec Sign Language (LSQ) and French.

includes embedding and teaching aspects of Deaf culture through-out P–12 education (e.g., identity development, Deaf epistemologies, understanding and acceptance of self and others). We believe that within multicultural education we must also integrate antiaudist, antibias, antiracist, antisexist, and antiableist education. This includes addressing injustices throughout the P–12 curriculum related to race, sex/gender, disability, power and privilege, and other minority groups (Christensen, 2017; English et al., 2018).

Heritage language/heritage language learner. In a given social environment, any language, whether signed or spoken, other than the majority language (e.g., English) that is connected to a minority community is a "heritage language" (Ortega, 2020). Immigrant, Indigenous, and minority community speakers learn their heritage languages at home, in their communities, and at school (e.g., Deaf and hearing children of Deaf adults [Codas]; Compton & Compton, 2014; Pichler et al., 2019). Deaf children who have hearing parents can be heritage language learners only if they learn ASL at home with their older Deaf siblings, in the signing communities, and at school (Isakson, 2018).

Translanguaging. We define "translanguaging" as the methodology for which Deaf children utilize and access different linguistic features via sign and print, plus various languages and communication systems (e.g., Augmentative and Alternative Communication [AAC]), in order to optimize communication and learning (De Meulder et al., 2019; García & Lin, 2017; Swanwick, 2017). García (2009) defines translanguaging as a multilingual approach that is centered on the overt discourse practices of emergent multilinguals. Teachers and their Deaf students use all of the languages in their linguistic repertoire to advance or develop literacy (Kurz & Kurz, in press). For example, Black Deaf students in the United States may navigate among ASL, Black ASL, and English to communicate ideas; Hmong Deaf students may switch between the use of ASL and Ho Chi Minh Sign Language to explain their ideas.

Deaf culture. We define "Deaf culture" as the set of beliefs and behaviors that reinforce the shared core values of Deaf communities (Holcomb, 2013) (e.g., Black, Latinx, Indigenous Deaf communities). These core values include full access to communication, information sharing, healthy identity formation, and self-determination. In the United States and parts of Canada, Deaf communities are largely influenced by the use of ASL and the additional languages, and common and unique experiences among diverse Deaf people.

American Sign Language. ASL is a natural language used by Deaf and hearing people in Deaf communities located in the United States, parts of Canada, and in various other countries (Valli & Lucas, 2000). ASL users have diverse gender, racial, ethnic, disability, cultural, linguistic, geographical, and socioeconomic backgrounds, and many of them have experienced oppression and discrimination. They also vary in their access to language resources, language dialects, linguistic creativity (language play, such as poems, rhymes, and slang words), and cultural funds of knowledge and skills, all of which are important assets to the wealth of diversity, variation, and dialects of ASL (e.g., Black ASL). Deaf people, including children of all ages, contribute to the evolution of ASL and its dialects. Because moving into a classroom and moving outside of a classroom doesn't change the kind of ASL used—or at least it should not—we choose not to use "social ASL" versus "academic ASL" to distinguish between ASL use in social or educational settings.

Multilingual strategies. We use the term "multilingual strategies" to expand on the previously used term "bilingual strategies," taking into consideration the multiple languages and cultures students bring to the classroom. We define multilingual strategies as strategies that support Deaf children's diverse linguistic repertoires of multiple languages (e.g., ASL, English, and other signed and written languages). However, we also recognize that teachers themselves are often not multilingual. While we encourage them to learn and use home and heritage languages (in addition to ASL and English) as much as possible, we also recognize that teachers are not typically fluent in all of the home languages used by their students. For example, a teacher can support vocabulary development for a Deaf student who moved to the United States from Colombia by incorporating Lengua de Señas Colombiana, or LSC (Colombian Sign Language) into lessons as a bridge to ASL and English (e.g., using pictures of her signing LSC words, ASL words, and printed English words). Further, research in Deaf education has been primarily based on bilingual strategies connecting ASL and English. There has been limited research related to multilingual teaching strategies in the United States and Canada.[4] Therefore, we choose to use the term multilingual strategies here, with the understanding that the focus specifically emphasizes research-based best practices for connecting ASL and English in the classroom, but with encouragement to consider additional languages as well.

Multimodal strategies. Modalities are the channels by which communication happens. These channels can be visual/manual (signed languages), auditory/oral (spoken languages), print (written languages), tactile (Protactile sign languages), among others. Here, we support the concept of a semiotic repertoire as explained by Kusters et al. (2017), wherein people combine multiple modalities for the purpose of ensuring positive communication environments with a variety of language-support partners.

We want to emphasize that multimodal strategies should be tailored to Deaf students' abilities to learn, not the teacher's preferences or abilities. Deaf students who do not use auditory input for learning, for example, should be provided with multiple modalities that optimize their learning channels (e.g., visual/manual, tactile, and kinesthetic). Teachers need to advocate for their Deaf students, such as stating on a student's Individual Education Plan (IEP) that the student's instruction is carried out in the most accessible modality/modalities.

KEY COMPONENTS OF A MULTILINGUAL DEAF EDUCATION TEACHER PREPARATION PROGRAM

Over the past several years, a group of 20 MLE-SIG representatives from bilingual teacher preparation programs systematically reviewed current program requirements, syllabi, content, and research related to bilingual education. The key components recommended here are the result of these activities. We begin by sharing recommendations for program coordinators, and follow with key components for multilingual teacher preparation programs.

The following recommendations are geared toward graduate teacher licensure programs, since the majority of Deaf education teacher preparation

---

4. For multilingual strategies used in Latin America, see Gerner de Garcia and Becker Karnopp (2016), and in other countries across the globe, see Wang and Andrews (2020).

programs are at the graduate level. However, we recognize that some programs offer teacher preparation at the undergraduate level, so we will make some specific notes for that where appropriate. Additionally, we take into consideration that most Deaf education licenses awarded are birth–21. It is important to also note that we recognize that each program will have to align with their individual state standards and state certification protocols. As a result, we encourage you to integrate these recommendations in whatever way works best for your program and state licensure requirements.

CONSIDERATIONS FOR PROGRAM COORDINATORS

Whether you are considering modifying your current program or doing a complete overhaul, the first step is making sure your faculty and instructors are qualified. Here are our minimal required and preferred recommendations for hiring faculty and instructors in the United States and parts of Canada:

- required: fluency in ASL and English
- required: minimum of 3 years P–12 teaching experience, preferably in a bilingual/multilingual Deaf education setting
- required: master's degree or higher in Deaf education, preferably from a bilingual/multilingual teacher preparation program
- preferred: Deaf faculty/instructors
- preferred: BIPOC faculty/instructors
- preferred: fluency in additional languages

When considering student recruitment, it is critical to recruit students who are BIPOC, Deaf, nontraditional, and/or teacher assistants. One way to increase recruitment is by including these characteristics as evaluation measures when seeking federal, state, or private funding. By preparing future BIPOC teachers we are also increasing the potential for future BIPOC faculty in Deaf education teacher preparation programs.

We strongly recommend that teacher candidates entering graduate Deaf education programs have a background in education (e.g., elementary, early childhood, special education, secondary) and/or academic content knowledge (e.g., mathematics, arts, science, Deaf studies, social studies, physical education, technology). Those students who do not have a background in education should take foundational education courses before taking Deaf education methods courses. We also recommend collaborating when possible with undergraduate programs in elementary/secondary and Deaf education. We encourage students to take their ASL I–IV (and beyond, where possible) classes in their undergraduate program or before graduate program admission.

Key Components

From our systematic review of current program syllabi and content and research related to bilingual education, we came up with a list of components that characterized a bilingual teacher preparation program. From there we narrowed down and identified seven key components we believe are essential in a quality *multilingual* program. We believe that by integrating these seven recommended components into your program, the number of graduates who are highly qualified to teach Deaf learners will increase. The seven components are as follows:

1. language competencies of teacher candidates
2. identity development, socioemotional health, and well-being
3. Deaf studies, social justice, and equity
4. multilingual instructional strategies
5. assessments of Deaf students in multiple languages
6. methods courses and teaching pedagogy
7. collaboration and resources

1. Language Competencies of Teacher Candidates

The first key component is related to language competencies that we expect teacher candidates to have upon entering a teacher preparation program. In order to facilitate their future students' language and academic content knowledge development, we believe these skills are critical for teachers to have themselves. When possible, we recommend that programs provide fluent language models in both ASL and English within their coursework.

Entrance Requirements for Teacher Preparation Programs. When teacher candidates are admitted to a teacher preparation program, we expect them to have a minimum proficiency in both ASL and written English. We recommend that students have at least taken ASL I–IV; they should also be proficient in conversational ASL. Some programs might attach an ASLPI score of "level 3" or SLPI score of "intermediate" as an admission requirement.[5]

We also recommend requiring a video submission as part of the application package. Within this submission, they would answer questions in ASL related to why they want to be accepted into a teacher preparation program and what they know about philosophies of Deaf education. Students should be prepared to take all of their Deaf education upper-level or graduate-level methods courses in ASL.

Students should also demonstrate proficiency in written English on their application (e.g., narrative, essay writing, research paper). That being said, a student should not be penalized for using a dialect of English (e.g., African American English).

We recognize that even though students may meet these requirements upon entrance, they may still need additional support throughout the program to advance their ASL and/or English skills. Instructors can scaffold these skills by modeling throughout each of their courses all of the multilingual/multimodal strategies we recommend, and consider providing mentors when possible.

ASL and English Linguistics. We recommend that each teacher preparation program includes at least one course on ASL and English comparative linguistics, and an additional course on the linguistics of signed languages. This would include teaching the phonology, morphology, syntax, and structure of each language; providing comparative study and application of language structures in the classroom; as well as providing students the opportunity to transcribe and analyze language samples of Deaf children in each language using discourse analysis theories. Ultimately, teacher candidates should be able to identify language goals for both ASL and written English (i.e., language arts).

2. Identity Development, Socioemotional Health, and Well-Being

The identity/well-being of teachers and facilitating identity development and well-being for Deaf students are often overlooked in teacher preparation programs. Teacher candidates should have an understanding of the implications and impact that language deprivation has on Deaf children's identity development and socioemotional well-being. Because children's sense of self

---

5. American Sign Language Proficiency Interview (ASPLI) and Sign Language Proficiency Interview (SLPI), respectively.

and others begins from birth, they may internalize whatever positive or negative messages they learn from an early age. It is also important teachers are familiar with trauma-informed curriculum; examining societal ignorance, assumptions, and definitions of proper behaviors. There are many instances of behavioral issues being mislabeled due to mistaken assumptions about Deaf students. Teachers should be aware of how to recognize potential cultural conflicts, communication breakdowns and frustrations, and cultural behaviors. Teachers should also be aware of the lasting impacts of language deprivation on communication and behaviors (Glickman & Hall, 2018; Gulati, 2018).

In order for teachers to be able to skillfully facilitate their student's identity development, they first must have a good awareness of their own identity: who they are, their privilege, their values, and who they want to be as a teacher. They then need to understand the complexities of having multiple and intersecting identities, as well as how to facilitate identity development in their future students.

Mindfulness practices can provide strategies for dealing with challenging emotions and difficult situations and conversations (Schonert-Reichl et al., 2015). Teachers can benefit along with their students by engaging in these practices (Neff & Germer, 2013). We recommend offering courses that cover identity and well-being, which can include some of these practices. However, even if you have a separate course it is important to integrate these concepts program-wide.

Self-Care/Mindfulness Practices for Teacher Candidates. We recommend incorporating self-care practices throughout your program so that teacher candidates begin to develop practices early on and have them in place before their first year of teaching. These foundational skills may help prevent teacher burnout (Roeser et al., 2013). Some recommendations for how to do this:

- Begin and end your class sessions with a short mindfulness activity. Have students take turns leading the activity.

- Integrate a self-care assignment into one or more of your courses. Ask the students to do some sort of self-care and reflect on their experience.

Self-Care Practices for Their Future Students. While it is important to facilitate all Deaf students' positive sense of self, awareness of others perspectives, and overall well-being, it is even more critical for those who have experienced trauma (e.g., language deprivation, racism, audism). Therefore, we also recommend the following practices be incorporated into teacher preparation programs, so that teacher candidates are ready to use them with their future students:

- invite Deaf presenters who are certified in yoga and/or mindfulness to demonstrate techniques in the classroom

- have students develop their own mindfulness videos in ASL (and additional languages) to incorporate into their classrooms

- incorporate activities in the classroom that facilitate identity development (e.g., art, drama, storytelling, and sign language multimedia)

- promote the importance of identity acceptance and a sense of belonging

- invite Deaf role models from diverse backgrounds to the classroom

- include children's books and media (e.g., videos, apps) with Deaf characters and in ASL

- discuss messages conveyed regarding portrayal of Deaf people in media and literature (with consideration of potential biases and stereotypes)

While these practices should be incorporated into teacher preparation programs, teacher candidates need to also see them applied in the classroom to better understand how they can integrate them in their future classrooms.

3. Deaf Studies, Social Justice,[6] and Equity

In schools for the Deaf, Deaf studies has sometimes been offered as a separate class. However, it is rarely infused across the curriculum, and when it is the focus, it is often not through the lens of a multicultural perspective. Curriculum needs to be transformative and more inclusive of all cultures; this applies to Deaf studies as well. As outlined in our theoretical framework (see Figure 2), it is time to expand this perspective to consider addressing the multiple identities that can intersect with one's Deaf identity (e.g., race, gen-

---

6. Since the writing of these guidelines, there have been conversations about terminology—restorative justice and transformative justice—in deaf education.

der, culture, disability; Bayley et al., 2019; McCaskill et al., 2011). Teacher candidates should know how to identify goals and objectives to target key standards of Deaf studies as aligned with the Deaf Culture Community of Wealth (Fleischer et al., 2020), and integrate this concept throughout the curriculum to ensure they are fostering equitable education. This includes:

- the history of Deaf people and ASL within the context of general history (e.g., Deaf people in the U.S. Civil War, Deaf people who lived in the British colonies in America, segregated schools for the Deaf and Black ASL)
- Deaf Gain, Deafhood, Deaf epistemologies
- Deaf communities (e.g., organizations such as National Black Deaf Advocates, Deaf people of diverse ethnic, race, geographic, and gender-based backgrounds)
- Deaf people in science, mathematics, history, literature, and other disciplines
- understanding and awareness of DeafSpace
- Deaf poetry, storytelling, and theater
- international and federal disability-related laws: Convention on the Rights of Persons With Disabilities (CRPD), Individuals With Disabilities Education Act (IDEA), Section 504 of the Rehabilitation Act of 1973, Americans With Disabilities Act (ADA)
- Deaf filmmaking, photography, newscasting, De'VIA
- languages and cultures of Deaf people around the world

Deaf students should have opportunities to discuss and role-play issues and solutions between teachers, families, and community members. This includes ways to communicate with families, and understanding varying perspectives on the topic.

We define the social justice competency "as both a process and a goal which includes the knowledge, skills, and dispositions needed to create learning environments that foster equitable participation of all groups while seeking to address and acknowledge issues of oppression, privilege, and power" (ACPA & NASPA, 2016, p. 28). Aligning with the aforementioned list of Deaf studies concepts to integrate across the curriculum, teacher candidates need to develop competencies in working with Deaf people to address issues of injustice, especially where access and marginalization are concerned. This includes incorporating antiaudist, antibias, antiracist, antisexist, and antiableist education (e.g., Derman-Sparks et al., 2020). We advocate for including the following areas related to social justice and equity that teacher candidates should know how to teach and integrate throughout the curriculum:

- social justice principles
- teaching about biases, lived experiences, and perspectives
- teaching about race, class, gender, sexuality, and disability
- teaching about power and privilege
- teaching about allyship and activism
- teaching about intersecting/multiple identities
- self-awareness, confidence, family pride, and positive individual and social (group) identities
- comfort and joy with human diversity; accurate language for human differences; and deep, caring human connections
- unfairness, language used to describe unfairness, and the negative impacts of unfairness
- empowerment and the skills to act, with others or alone, against prejudice or discrimination
- equity in education, the workplace, and courtrooms (mock trials)
- communication with families
- involvement of Deaf adults from diverse backgrounds in the classroom
- accessible multimedia resources to present varying perspectives
- consideration of technology availability in homes for Deaf students

4. Multilingual Instructional Strategies

Teacher candidates must graduate with the knowledge and ability to implement multilingual strategies across all content areas and P–12 grade levels (i.e., mathematics, reading, writing, language arts, ASL, Deaf studies, science, and social studies) for both in person and virtual learning. This includes providing ASL and English (and home/heritage languages when possible) in curriculum, instruction, and assessment, and having a "toolkit" of strategies that can be used to:

- connect languages (ASL, English, and home/heritage languages) to one another
- write lesson plans with targeted language and academic content goals, objectives, procedures, and evaluations
- teach strategies specific to subject areas
- integrate cognitive strategies across multiple subjects (e.g., thinking maps, KWL chart, concept mapping, theme-based learning)
- integrate language modalities (e.g., signed, viewed, spoken, written) across the curriculum
- differentiate instruction for varying modality levels, language levels, and educational settings
- differentiate instruction for students from multicultural/multilingual families
- differentiate instruction for immigrant and refugee families
- develop materials in both ASL and English for varying reading, writing, and language levels
- integrate technology into instruction including media in ASL, apps/tablet, internet, and vlogs
- develop materials for online learning utilizing most current software (e.g., online video platforms)
- tap into the funds of knowledge that children and their families can bring from home (González et al., 2005). For example, Latinx families providing storytelling, cooking classes, or sharing other aspects of their cultures

Because of language deprivation and lack of access to fluent ASL models or Deaf peers, Deaf students often don't have language to attach to their experiences (Hopper, 2011; Meeks, 2020; Olivia et al., 2016). As a result, it is important for P–12 Deaf education teachers to create welcoming environments where incidental learning is possible. Upon graduating, teacher candidates should be aware of ways to provide activities and experiences for incidental learning across the grade span. This includes opportunities for peer interaction through field trips, small group and cooperative learning, and structured and unstructured play. Most importantly, teachers need to create an environment of positive, unfettered access to signed languages (Humphries, 2013). That means signing amongst each other and refusing to speak on school campuses or in online learning environments, unless the speech is made completely accessible to any Deaf person who may encounter it.

It is important for instructors of methods courses to model best practice strategies. Call attention to the strategies as instructors use them to heighten the teacher candidate's awareness of when and how they may be implemented. This will help them begin to make connections both within and across courses throughout your program.

5. Assessments of Deaf Students in Multiple Languages

Teacher candidates should graduate from their program with an understanding of formal and informal assessments used to evaluate Deaf students' language and literacy skills, and the positives and negatives of each. They should have an understanding of the concerns with reliability and validity of standardized assessments for Deaf students and how to administer them. Assessments are often not appropriate for Deaf students, particularly considering cultural and linguistic backgrounds. They can also be time consuming to administer. Thus, it is important that teacher candidates have a strong knowledge of informal assessments such as checklists, portfolios, or language samples. These should be integrated throughout multiple courses, and students should have plenty of opportunities to review and/or administer assessments.

Teacher candidates should have the opportunity to review and participate in the development of goals and objectives for IEP (Individual Education Plan) and IFSP (Individual Family Service Plan). They should understand the process as well. Within each lesson plan that students write they should include how they will assess the objectives for those lessons. Students should have multiple opportunities in each methods course to develop and implement assessment measures.

The following are examples of both formal and informal language assessments:

- American Sign Language Phonological Awareness Test (ASL-PAT):

The ASL-PAT (McQuarrie & Cundy, 2019) is a computer-based test designed to assess children's (ages 4–13 years) awareness of the phonological structure of ASL (i.e., the sublexical parameters of handshape [HS], location [L], and movement [M]). It measures a child's ability to identify phonological similarity relations (i.e., discriminate minimal contrasts) in signs across three comparison conditions: signs with three (HS + L + M); two (HS + M, L + M, or HS + L); or one (HS, M, or L) shared parameter(s).

- ASL Expressive Skills Test (ASL-EST): The ASL-EST (Enns et al., 2019) assesses children's (ages 4–13 years) narrative ASL abilities through an elicitation task using a language-free story on video. Specifically, the child watches the video and then spontaneously retells the story, including answering three comprehension questions. The child's responses are video recorded and analyzed according to specific scoring guidelines focused on narrative content/structure (events in the story and story development), as well as ASL grammar, including spatial verbs, agreement verbs, aspect, manner, and role shift.

- ASL Receptive Skills Test (ASL-RST): The ASL-RST (Enns et al., 2013) measures children's (ages 3–13 years) comprehension of ASL morphology and syntax. It assesses eight grammatical structures: (a) number/distribution; (b) noun-verb distinction; (c) negation; (d) spatial verbs; (e) handling classifiers; (f) size-and-shape classifiers; (g) conditional clauses; and (h) role shift.

- American Sign Language Assessment Inventory (ASL-AI): The ASL-AI (Hoffmeister et al., 2014) is a web-based test for Deaf children (ages 4–18 years) consisting of 12 tasks. It targets conversational abilities, academic language knowledge, language comprehension, analogical reasoning, and metalinguistic skills.

- Visual Communication and Sign Language (VCSL) Checklist for Signing Children: The VCSL Checklist (Simms et al., 2013) is a standardized measure of ASL acquisition for young children (ages birth–5) in the United States. It monitors children's sign language acquisition and helps determine if children are developmentally on track.

- MacArthur-Bates Communicative Development Inventory for American Sign Language (ASL-CDI): The ASL-CDI is a communication assessment that was adapted for ASL (Anderson & Reilly, 2002). It is a checklist for families to fill out and identify ASL vocabulary that their Deaf child understands and produces. As of this writing, ASL-CDI 2.0 is now available in a beta version (Caselli et al., 2020).

- Some informal reading assessments include reading and writing checklists and informal reading inventories (French, 1999).

- When possible, teacher candidates should also seek informal and formal assessment tools to evaluate home and heritage language development.

6. Methods Courses and Teaching Pedagogy

Teacher candidates must take methods courses that cover the breadth of each of the first five components for all age groups covered by their license—with some being birth–21. Even students who plan on teaching high school science could someday be placed in a preschool setting; therefore, all teacher candidates must have foundational knowledge of content areas across the age span. The strategy list described previously should be incorporated in multiple ways, and integrated into multiple methods courses specific to teaching Deaf students. This section will provide examples of methods courses you could have within your program.

Academic Content Through ASL (Viewing/Signing) Methods. We recommend a course that requires teacher candidates to develop and teach lesson plans across content areas and grade levels, with the focus being on evaluating not only their ability to develop lessons and teach effectively using multilingual strategies, but also to evaluate their ability to teach using ASL. They should also be able to evaluate Deaf students' understanding of academic concepts expressed through ASL. This includes the understanding of and ability to implement the following best practices for teaching across grade levels:

- using viewing comprehension strategies in teaching

- teaching ASL word study and fluency

- signing fluency strategies (e.g., grade-level based signing)

- using ASL rhythm and rhyme to target ASL phonological awareness in early childhood

- integrating ASL poetry and literature across the curriculum

- connecting background knowledge to content in ASL

- comparing and contrasting grammatical structures in ASL and English

- bridging ASL and English (and other home/heritage languages when possible) in all academic content

- teaching translation skills

- developing and using curriculum materials, instructional strategies, and assessment tools in ASL

- incorporating and connecting to cultures and funds of knowledge across the curriculum (e.g., Deaf epistemology)

The ability to not only sign abstract and academic concepts, but also teach these concepts across the curriculum, has often been overlooked in teacher preparation programs. Teacher candidates need opportunities to consider linguistic features of ASL for language functions that are part of the classroom routine, including the ability to sign appropriate grade-level and abstract higher-level concepts accurately (e.g., algebraic equations, gravity, the water cycle, poetry).

Early Language/Literacy Acquisition and Development Methods. One area that is often overlooked is *emergent* literacy development. Some educators believe that young children first must have a strong language foundation before being exposed to print. Because of this, emergent literacy often gets neglected. However, there is so much children can learn about print before they learn to read or write (e.g., concepts of print, that print carries meaning, print in the environment). What happens during early childhood impacts all future learning for all content areas. It is critical that teacher candidates understand the whole child approach and the importance of a language and literacy foundation (see Figure 1), and recognize that all children are able to learn about print before age 5. Further, all teachers, regardless of the grade or subject they teach, must understand how children acquire language and develop literacy from birth. They must also be able to evaluate and recognize the gaps and strengths in their students' language and literacy skills.

We recommend that teacher preparation programs include at least one course on each of the following:

- Early intervention: This course would address early identification, assessment, family-centered interdisciplinary servicing, and program development for Deaf infants, toddlers, and their families. This includes specific methods and procedures for working with families, including facilitating language, literacy, numeracy, and early interactive communication. The role of Deaf mentors should also be addressed.

- Language/literacy development/assessment birth–5: We recommend a course or competencies that captures both language and literacy goals so that students can see how these align with each other. This includes discussing language milestones for both ASL and English and an understanding of the impacts of language deprivation on academics, social-emotional skills, etc.

- Preschool methods: Further, because we are talking about multilingual strategies, it is important that literacy is not taught as a subject separate from language, particularly at the early childhood stages. Early childhood education provides a foundation for language, literacy, numeracy, and identity development, and all teachers should understand and be familiar with these key concepts and methods. This also includes antibias education for young children (Derman-Sparks et al., 2020).

Reading and Writing Methods (K–12). This course (or courses, as reading and writing methods could be split into multiple courses) should integrate reading and writing methods, and provide teacher candidates multiple opportunities to develop lesson plans and teach them for feedback. Some key strategies to cover here are: readers'/writers' workshop, interactive writing strategies, shared reading, guided reading, reading "aloud," differentiating instruction, and modifying materials based on reading, writing, and language levels. They should also have the opportunity to practice writing and implementing mini lessons and unit plans.

Another recommended course is one where teacher candidates learn how they can support adolescent literacy development in ASL and English for Deaf students, especially for those in grades 6–12. They would learn about various language and literacy instructional methods and how to incorporate literacy instruction into all content area classrooms (e.g., math, history, science, Deaf studies, in middle school or high school). This course would also cover both written and signed language academic papers, the latter being similar to academic writing (Shaw & Thumann, 2012).

Content Methods (K–12). These courses should provide opportunities to develop and teach lessons for the following subjects: mathematics, social studies, Deaf studies, and science. Ideally, programs would offer separate methods courses in each subject.

Teacher candidates should have multiple opportunities to practice how to integrate reading/writing/ASL into each of the content areas. This is also a good place to discuss the importance of integrating informational texts across the curriculum. Integrating technology is another good topic to include in this class. Students should also have the opportunity to practice developing an integrated unit plan that covers all topics "live" and through online learning. They should also be given opportunities to practice developing and modifying materials based on a Deaf student's reading/writing/ASL levels. Methods for transition could also be covered here or as a separate course.

Deaf With Disabilities/Disabled Deaf Communities. This course should provide opportunities for students to develop lessons and teach Deaf students with disabilities (e.g., DeafBlind, autism, attention-deficit/hyperactivity disorder, emotional/behavioral disorders). This includes practice developing social stories, using assistive technologies, writing a behavior intervention plan, reviewing an IEP, and developing lessons related to IEP objectives.

Additional Things to Consider. In addition to methods courses, students should also have courses that cover foundational knowledge of Deaf education. This includes understanding federal and state laws (e.g., ADA), laws around IEP/IFSP, advocacy, adaptation, accommodation and accessibility, behavior intervention plans, early intervention, newborn screening, audiology measures, and the history of Deaf education.

Finally, given the recent events that have transpired with the COVID-19 pandemic, it is critical that all teacher candidates are familiar with developing content and material appropriate for online learning. Each of the above methods courses should include the use of technology. Teacher candidates should effectively include and implement technology in the classroom, in online settings, and within lesson plans, including media in ASL, apps/iPad, internet, vlogs, and online learning software.

Requirements for Teacher Candidates Prior to Graduation. Prior to graduating, teacher candidates should demonstrate proficiency in effectively teaching content-area concepts in ASL and English across the P–12 grade span. This includes Deaf studies, ASL, reading/writing, language arts, science, social studies, and mathematics. Teacher candidates should also demonstrate the ability to navigate between languages, including demonstrating multilingual strategies for connecting ASL and written English (and other home/heritage languages). This should happen through observations during field placements and evaluations during student teaching both by the cooperating/ mentoring teacher and the faculty supervisor, as well as in the culminating language and teacher evaluations (these can be embedded within methods courses or as stand-alone evaluations).

Deaf Education Language and Teaching Evaluations. We do not believe measures like ASLPI and SLPI are sufficient for evaluating a teacher candidate's ability to use ASL to teach academic concepts. Instead, we recommend teacher candidates be evaluated using a Deaf education teaching evaluation. It will evaluate not only how well the candidate is able to use ASL to teach academic concepts across the content areas, but also how well they model multilingual teaching strategies.

There are of course many ways to evaluate teaching skills. For example, over a 2–3 hour period, teacher candidates could develop and implement lessons or microteaching sessions in their choice of subject area. We suggest allowing them to have approximately 1 hour to prepare for all subjects. They will then teach them "live" for about 10–15 minutes per subject (and a portion of this could be "live" in online settings as well). They are expected to demonstrate skills on the spot that have been integrated throughout the program (e.g., connecting ASL to English, defining vocabulary, demonstrating abstract concepts in ASL and being able to break them down, providing differentiated instruction, classroom management). During the lessons, the panel of evaluators (e.g., teachers in the program, teachers in the community) act as students. We recommend each candidate teach the following:

- science
- social studies

- reading aloud

- grammar lessons in both languages

- teaching mathematical story problems

- engaging students' Deaf identity through a book with a Deaf character

- issues and solutions (e.g., given a mock role play between teacher/ student or teacher/family to address issues using advocacy strategies through an antiracist/antibias lens)

We then suggest having two separate evaluation rubrics: one to evaluate their ability to frame academic concepts using both languages, and the other to evaluate their teaching skills. While we do not expect them to be perfect, it does allow for us to see how well they have internalized the strategies they have learned and are able to produce them on the spot. We prefer on the spot because we want to see their ASL skills "live" as they would be in a real classroom. Alternatively, you could do a mix of on the spot lessons and prepared lessons and compare them. Another consideration is providing opportunities for them to practice teaching lessons in both groups and in one-on-one settings. Regardless of which approach, teacher candidates should be then asked to reflect on their microteaching performance and describe what went well and what they would do differently, particularly in regards to their language use and teaching strategies.

Summary of Recommendations for Key Courses/Content. Upon graduation, teacher candidates should have had multiple opportunities to learn and practice teaching methods in multiple educational subjects, settings, and grade levels. We understand that program requirements vary, and the ability to require specific courses and/or the number of courses varies within each program/university. As a result, it is not possible to have a standardized course list across teacher preparation programs. That being said, here is a list of key courses and content that we recommend for programs aspiring to align with a multilingual perspective for Deaf education:

- ASL/English linguistics and application

- language and literacy development and assessment (including language deprivation)

- methods for teaching early childhood

- methods for teaching reading/writing across the curriculum
- methods for teaching content areas (including Deaf studies, math, science, social studies, reading/writing/language arts)
- application of teaching ASL academic concepts across the curriculum
- identity development, cultural diversity, and well-being
- social justice, advocacy, and laws
- behavior and classroom management
- legal aspects of working with ADA, IEP/IFSP writing, and due process
- Deaf with disabilities
- bimodal practices
- early intervention
- current research and trends in Deaf education
- transition (high school and after): advocacy skills and life skills
- practicum (we propose having at least three practicum experiences at varying grade levels, subjects, and educational settings)

If possible, teacher candidates should have their full-time, 15-week student teaching practicum (or two 8-week student teaching assignments) at a school for the Deaf.

7. Collaboration and Resources

Collaboration between teacher preparation programs and birth–21 Deaf education programs is an important aspect of not only improving teacher preparation, but bringing resources into birth–21 programs. Members of the MLE-SIG have identified mutual benefits that will result from collaborating. One of the benefits is preservice teacher candidates having increased opportunities for interaction with Deaf adults and Deaf children in educational settings. These interactions will provide teacher candidates with experiences that will support them in achieving language proficiency prior to being the teacher of record for Deaf children. Another benefit is the opportunity for teacher candidates to see skilled teachers in action, and witness successful and proficient implementation of multilingual educational pedagogy. In the case where a preservice teacher candidate may be working closely with a mentor, they may also have the option to set short- and medium-term goals for improvement, which can be evaluated and supported by the mentor.

In addition to benefits for teacher candidates, schools and programs serving Deaf students ages birth–21 will also see benefits from increased collaboration with universities. Specifically, these schools and programs will have better opportunities to recruit promising teacher candidates into the workforce. This will also allow schools to have a hand in the kind of instruction that teacher candidates see and learn during their training. Teachers may also benefit from learning about newly studied approaches to Multilingual Deaf Education that teacher candidates study during their university training.

The simplest way to begin collaborating is to reach out to local Deaf educational settings for practicum and student teaching placements. Students should have varied placement so they have at least one experience in each age setting (i.e., early childhood, elementary, middle school/high school/transition). In addition to age group experiences, students should also have experiences in varied educational settings. We recommend they have at least one experience at a school for the Deaf and that their student teaching placement is in a bilingual/multilingual setting. That being said, we believe it is important for teacher candidates to see what happens within and learn from other settings as well (e.g., self-contained, itinerant). Due to each of these factors, it is important to form partnerships and collaborations with multiple and varying educational settings for Deaf students.

Guest Lecturers/Adjunct Faculty. The collaborative relationship between local school programs and teacher training programs can be beneficial in other ways as well. For example, you can identify expert teachers in each content area and invite them as guest lecturers in methods courses, particularly for content areas for which there is not enough faculty expertise at the university. The university could reach out to an expert math teacher(with consideration for BIPOC and Deaf expert teachers), for instance, who can come and model a lesson, or demonstrate math vocabulary in ASL (they should be compensated for their contributions). You can arrange to observe their classes as well.

Classroom Projects/Mock Lessons. One idea for providing opportunities for your students to practice teaching lessons in a real classroom setting prior to student teaching is by partnering with local programs so teacher candidates can go in their cohort groups to plan and teach a lesson. In this situation, the classroom teacher is involved limitedly or only as a proctor, and the faculty instructor observes the candidates teaching the lesson. By having your whole class there together, they can observe and evaluate each other. This offers an opportunity for them to practice classroom management as well. If it's not realistic to go to a local school, another idea is to invite Deaf students from the local schools to come to your university classes for a mock lesson. This may work depending on what time of the day you offer your classes. If it is during the day, it could also be a win-win in that the K–12 students can see what a local university campus is like and learn about post-secondary education opportunities. If you are unable to partner with local programs due to distance, as a last resort you can invite students in beginning ASL courses to pretend they are students. This isn't quite the same, but it does allow for teacher candidates to practice with varying language levels, with the biggest difference being these students would already have a strong L1 (e.g., English).

Cohosting Training or Workshop Opportunities. Reach out to local programs to see how you can collaborate in hosting training or workshop opportunities that would benefit both your teacher candidates as well as teachers in the field. For example, if someone is thinking of bringing a presenter in from out of state, pool your resources together for planning and budgeting, and work together to host a workshop. Or for any event that you are already planning, consider inviting teachers/administrators from local programs. Stay connected and communicate with one another so you know when any local events are happening.

Stakeholder Groups. Invite teachers, administrators, and families with Deaf children to serve on your program's advisory committee or stakeholder group. You can share what is going on in your program and your needs for student recruitment, practicum placements, and faculty, and at the same time plan any training/workshop events as mentioned previously. It is important to involve families of Deaf children in these groups.

Collaborating With Community Individuals, Organizations, and Agencies. Within courses, teacher candidates should be provided with recommendations for ways they can collaborate with the community. This includes not only Deaf communities, but Deaf people from other diverse communities (e.g., Black, Latinx, Somalian, Hmong, LGBTQIA+ communities). We suggest inviting representatives from diverse Deaf community groups into the classroom to share their experiences, and provide suggestions for modifying curriculum or working with families from diverse backgrounds. You can have panel presentations, inviting different people for each class. You can also create a database of local presenters and then identify which of your courses they might be a good fit to come and present for. It is nice to have a pool of possible presenters for each class in case someone is not available. If you do not have a large local Deaf community or live near a Deaf school, you can invite people to present via a video meeting app.

Encourage teacher candidates to collaborate with local community agencies, such as local early intervention organizations (e.g., Deaf mentors, Hands and Voices, Deaf community agencies) or a school for the Deaf in the neighborhood. Invite representatives from these agencies to present to your students about the services they provide to the state. Teacher candidates could also volunteer for these agencies during local events, workshops, or conferences.

Families. You can collaborate with families of Deaf children in multiple ways:

- invite them to share their experiences as part of a panel discussion
- invite them to workshops/training hosted by your program
- connect your students with families to build relationships

Teacher candidates should practice and develop strategies for how best to communicate with families across the grade span. This can include extended family members, in addition to parents, caregivers, or immediate family.

Alumni. Maintaining relationships with your former students after graduation is a great way to seek partnerships. They could become great mentors to your teacher candidates as their philosophy/instructional strategies align with your program. Consider inviting these former students to be a part of your stakeholder groups, or to serve as cooperating teachers to host your teacher candidates for both field placement experiences and student teaching. We also suggest inviting them back to your courses to share their experiences in the field and/or provide feedback for your students.

Other Organizations and Conferences. Partnering with professional organizations is one way that may improve the pool of teacher candidates. You also could network with interpreter training programs to recruit graduates of their programs who are interested in education, have an undergraduate degree in interpreting, and possess strong language skills. Partnering with community organizations like the state and local Deaf community associations will also increase opportunities for students to become involved and connected to leaders in Deaf organizations. Invite members of these organizations to your courses to share their experiences. Partner with national organizations like the National Association of the Deaf, National Black Deaf Advocates, Council de Manos, and Sacred Circle to invite them to share resources. When possible, we encourage teacher candidates to attend local, state, and national Deaf-related conferences while they are in school.

Collaborating on Research. Partnering across universities and with P–12 programs to undertake research is important. As the need for high quality research in Deaf education continues to grow, pooling resources, knowledge bases, and perspectives/beliefs/backgrounds will allow for more nuanced studies. It is clear we need *collaborative* research and dissemination across universities, colleges, and P–12 programs on best practices for multilingual teacher preparation in areas of pedagogy, dispositions, student qualifications, teaching competencies, field experiences (i.e., practicum and student teaching), and program impacts on student learning.

Finding and Sharing Resources. We recognize that it is not possible for teacher preparation programs to teach teacher candidates everything. However, they should graduate with the knowledge of where and who to approach for resources they may need in the future. Sharing resources between other teacher preparation programs and local communities helps build relationships between those involved (e.g., contacts for local and national agencies and organizations, conferences, events). The development of a database of such resources can be shared with teacher candidates during and after their program.

NEXT STEPS AND TIPS FOR TRANSITIONING
Next Steps

If you are interested in either supporting multilingual teacher preparation programs or transitioning your program to align with a multilingual perspective, we encourage you to become members of the MLE-SIG[7] and at-

---

7. We are in the process of proposing a name change for the MLE-SIG to align with a Multilingual Deaf Education perspective.

tend the annual ACEDHH conference. This will be a way we can continue to share and grow resources to support you in the process. Here are some action steps we plan to take as the MLE-SIG to support programs in implementing the guidelines:

- MLE-SIG website: While the MLE-SIG has already established a new website located on the ACEDHH website, one of the next steps to support existing and new teacher preparation programs in becoming multilingual is to expand on resources within the SIG website. Our hope is that members will utilize the SIG website as a place to share resources.

- MLE-SIG event at the annual ACEDHH conference: The SIG will continue their annual day-long event adjacent to the main ACEDHH conference for collaborative projects, including sharing and building additional resources such as course syllabi, teacher modeling videos, and the latest research findings.

- equity of BIPOC: The MLE-SIG aims to increase BIPOC representation and membership at the annual conference to ensure their perspectives are represented in our SIG actions, policies, presentations, and publications.

- developing evaluative tools: The MLE-SIG aims to develop and share multiple options for tools that can be used to evaluate the quality of Multilingual Deaf Education teacher preparation programs.

TIPS FOR TRANSITIONING

Ready to align your teacher preparation program with a Multilingual Deaf Education perspective? Here are some tips for getting started:

- review your state licensure requirements for standards
- review your university/college requirements for standards, credit limits, etc.
- review your department/college procedures for minor versus major course revisions
- review your department/college procedures for creating a new course

- review your department/college procedures for course revisions versus program revisions
- review faculty vita, loads, and responsibilities to determine who will teach which courses

Program Changes

Full program changes can include major/minor course revisions, and revisions to program goals, admission requirements (e.g., ASL skills), and program evaluations. Keep in mind that if you are making extensive program changes, some university/college requirements ask that you wait to submit all requests at one time. However, if you are only changing a few courses you might not have to submit a full program change. Some colleges require approval from curriculum committees. We recommend when possible to revise courses you already have in place. This can help you transition more smoothly, and is typically less time consuming than getting a new course proposed and approved.

Course Revisions

Sometimes programs separate language from literacy. Since key strategies connect language to written print, we do not recommend this for multilingual programs. For example, if you have one language and one literacy course that is currently P–12 and you want to split it into two courses, Early Childhood Language/Literacy and P–12 Literacy Methods, you wouldn't need to create two new courses. You could do the following:

- modify the current literacy course by taking out the early childhood parts. This could consist of major or minor revisions, depending on your university's requirements.
- create one new course for early childhood.

Unlike minor course revisions, which may only need to be reviewed at the program/department level, major course revisions usually require review by the college curriculum committee. When revising courses, there should be a focus on materials that come from Deaf and/or BIPOC scholars.

Creating a New Course

There is no need to reinvent the wheel! If you are creating a new course (e.g., Multilingual Methods for Teaching Academic Content) we recommend first reaching out to the MLE-SIG for a sample syllabus. This can help you not only with content but with your standards as well. Please note that standards for each course will vary based on the guidelines set by your university, state, and in some cases, the Council on Education of the Deaf (CED). Importantly, some universities already include statements regarding antibias, anti racist principles. If yours does not, this will be something you will want to include. While it is critical to integrate antiaudist, antibias, antiracist, and social justice principles throughout your program, you may also decide to have a separate course as well (e.g., Identity Development, Intersectionality, and Social Justice). When creating new courses, there should be a focus on materials that come from Deaf and/or BIPOC scholars.

You also may want to consider whether you want to include an online component to your course (e.g., blended learning). If you do decide to add this component, we recommend the course be designed to emphasize genuine learning experiences so teacher candidates have opportunities to learn, interact, and collaborate with each other.

Deaf Education Teaching Evaluation

In regards to our recommendation for a Deaf education teaching evaluation (see pp. 30–31), consider whether you want to embed this into one of your courses or make it a standalone credit or exam This can take substantial time to administer and evaluate, so you might want to consider this when determining the duties, loads, and responsibilities of your faculty.

CONCLUSION

It has been over 30 years since foundational principles for bilingual Deaf education programs were first recommended. Here we have attempted to update and expand on those principles to provide guidelines for Deaf education teacher preparation programs that reflect the current needs and trends of Multilingual Deaf Education. We recognize that each state has their own standards and requirements for licensure. These guidelines provide recommendations for key components to incorporate into multilingual teacher preparation programs, while also allowing each program the flexibility to incorporate the recommendations in the way that works best for their program. It is our hope that faculty and administrators in teacher preparation programs will use the guidelines to improve upon an existing bilingual program, transition a program to become multilingual, or create new multilingual programs. Finally, we want to acknowledge that Multilingual Deaf Education is fluid, as we are always learning and seeking out new ways to improve. Ultimately, these guidelines can lead us as we continue to take steps toward providing equitable education. With this, we hope we can work together more collaboratively to improve the lives and educational experiences of all Deaf students across North America. It is time for change. We hope you will join us on this journey.

REFERENCES

Anderson, D., & Reilly, J. (2002). The MacArthur Communicative Development Inventory: Normative data for American Sign Language. *Journal of Deaf Studies and Deaf Education, 7*(2), 83–106.

Bayley, R., Lucas, C., Hill, J., & McCaskill, C. (2019). The sociolinguistic ramifications of social injustice: The case of Black ASL. In R. Blake & I. Buchstaller (Eds.), *The Routledge companion to the work of John R. Rickford* (pp. 133–141). Routledge.

Burke, M. L. (2014). *Ableism in the Deaf community and the field of Deaf studies: Through the eyes of a DeafDisabled person* [Unpublished master's thesis]. Gallaudet University.

Cannon, J. E., Guardino, C., & Gallimore, E. (2016). A new kind of heterogeneity: What we can learn from d/Deaf and hard of hearing multilingual learners. *American Annals of the Deaf, 161*(1), 8–16.

Caselli, N. K., Lieberman, A. M., & Pyers, J. E. (2020). The ASL-CDI 2.0: an updated, normed adaptation of the MacArthur Bates Communicative Development Inventory for American Sign Language. *Behavior Research Methods, 52*, 1–14.

Christensen, K. (Ed.). (2017). *Educating Deaf students in a multicultural world*. DawnSignPress.

College Student Educators International (ACPA) & Student Affairs Administrators in Higher Education (NASPA). (2016). *ACPA/NASPA professional competencies rubrics*.

Compton, S., & Compton, S. (2014). American Sign Language as a heritage language. In T. G. Wiley, J. K. Peyton, D. Christian, S. C. K. Moore, & N. Liu (Eds.), *Handbook of heritage, community, and Native American languages in the United States: Research, policy, and educational practice* (pp. 272–283). Routledge.

Conference of Educational Administrators of Schools and Programs for the Deaf (CEASD). (2020, December 21). *Letter to President-Elect Joseph Biden and Vice President-Elect Kamala Harris*.

Conference of Educational Administrators of Schools and Programs for the Deaf (CEASD) & National Association for the Deaf (NAD). (2018, July 30). *Letter to Johnny Collett, Assistant Secretary, Office of Special Education and Rehabilitative Services, US Department of Education.*

Crenshaw, K., Gotanda, N., Peller, G., & Thomas, K. (Eds.). (1995). *Critical Race Theory: The key writings that formed the movement.* The New Press.

De Meulder, M., Kusters, A., Moriarty, E., & Murray, J. J. (2019). Describe, don't prescribe: The practice and politics of translanguaging in the context of deaf signers. *Journal of Multilingual and Multicultural Development, 40*(10), 892–906.

Denninger, M. (2017). Lesbian, gay, bisexual, and transgender deaf students: Invisible and underserved. In K. Christensen (Ed.), *Educating Deaf students in a multicultural world* (pp. 271–294). DawnSignPress.

Derman-Sparks, L., Edwards, J. O., & Goins, C. M. (2020). *Anti-bias education for young children and ourselves* (2nd ed.). The National Association for the Education of Young Children.

Dunn, L. M., & Anderson, G. B. (2019). Examining the intersectionality of Deaf identity, race/ethnicity, and diversity through a Black Deaf lens. In I. W. Leigh & C. A. O'Brien (Eds.), *Deaf identities: Exploring new frontiers* (pp. 279–304). Oxford University Press.

English, D., Rendina, H. J., & Parsons, J. T. (2018). The effects of intersecting stigma: A longitudinal examination of minority stress, mental health, and substance use among Black, Latino, and multiracial gay and bisexual men. *Psychology of Violence, 8*(6), 669.

Enns, C., Zimmer, K., Boudreault, P., Rabu, S., & Broszeit, C. (2013). *American Sign Language Receptive Skills Test.* Northern Signs Research.

Enns, C., Zimmer, K., Broszeit, C., & Rabu, S. (2019). *American Sign Language Expressive Skills Test.* Northern Signs Research.

Fleischer, F., Narr, R. F., & Garrow, W. (2020). Why deaf education matters: Including deaf students with disabilities. *Odyssey: New Directions in Deaf Education, 21,* 52–55.

French, M. (1999). Starting with assessment: A developmental approach to deaf children's literacy. Pre-College National Mission Programs, Gallaudet University.

Gallaudet Research Institute. (2013). *Regional and national summary report of data from the 2011-2012 annual survey of deaf and hard of hearing children and youth.* Gallaudet University.

Gárate-Estes, M., Lawyer, G. L., & García-Fernández, C. (in press). The U.S. Latinx Deaf communities: Situating and envisioning the transformative potential of translanguaging. In M. T. Sánchez & O. García (Eds.), *Transformative translanguaging espacios in bilingual education: U.S. Latinx bilingual children rompiendo fronteras*. Multilingual Matters.

García, O. (2009). Bilingualism and translanguaging. In O. García (Ed.), *Bilingual education in the 21st century: A global perspective* (pp. 42–72). Oxford.

García, O., & Lin, A. M. (2017). Translanguaging in bilingual education. In O. García, A. M. Y. Lin, & S. May (Eds.), *Bilingual and multilingual education* (pp. 117–130). Springer.

García-Fernández, C. (2020). Intersectionality and autoethnography: Deaf-Blind, DeafDisabled, Deaf and Hard of Hearing-Latinx children are the future. *Journal Committed to Social Change on Race and Ethnicity, 6*(1), 41–67.

Gerner de Garcia, B., & Becker Karnopp, L. (Eds.). (2016). *Change and promise: Bilingual deaf education and deaf culture in Latin America*. Gallaudet University Press.

Glickman, N., & Hall, W. (2018). *Language deprivation and deaf mental health*. Routledge.

González, N., Moll, L. C., & Amanti, C. (Eds.). (2005). *Funds of knowledge: Theorizing practices in households, communities, and classrooms*. Routledge.

Gulati, S. (2018). Language deprivation syndrome. In N. Glickman & W. Hall (Eds.), *Language deprivation and deaf mental health* (pp. 24–53). Routledge.

Hall, M. L., Hall, W. C., & Caselli, N. K. (2019). Deaf children need language, not (just) speech. *First Language, 39*(4), 367–395.

Hall, W. C., Levin, L. L., & Anderson, M. L. (2017). Language deprivation syndrome: A possible neurodevelopmental disorder with sociocultural origins. *Social Psychiatry and Psychiatric Epidemiology, 52*(6), 761–776.

Hoffmeister, R. J., Caldwell-Harris, C. L., Henner, J., Benedict, R., Fish, S., Rosenburg, P., & Novogrodsky, R. (2014). *The American Sign Language Assessment Instrument (ASLAI): Progress report and preliminary findings* [Working paper]. Center for the Study of Communication and the Deaf.

Holcomb, T. K. (2013). *Introduction to American Deaf culture.* Oxford University Press.

Hopper, M. (2011). *Positioned as bystanders: Deaf students' experiences and perceptions of informal learning phenomena* [Unpublished doctoral dissertation]. University of Rochester.

Humphries, T. (2013). Schooling in American Sign Language: A paradigm shift from a deficit model to a bilingual model in deaf education. *Berkeley Review of Education, 4*(1), 7–33.

Isakson, S. K. (2018). The case for heritage ASL instruction for hearing heritage signers. *Sign Language Studies, 18*(3), 385–411.

Johnson, R. E., Liddell, S. K., & Erting, C. J. (1989). *Unlocking the curriculum: Principles for achieving access in deaf education* [Gallaudet Research Institute Working Paper 89-3]. Gallaudet University.

Kuntze, M., & Golos, D. (2021). Revisiting rethinking literacy. In C. Enns, J. Henner, & L. McQuarrie (Eds.), *Discussing bilingualism in deaf children: Essays in honor of Robert Hoffmeister* (pp. 99–112). Routledge.

Kurz, C. A., & Kurz, K. (in press). Infusing ASL in academic settings. In E. A. Winston & S. B. Fitzmaurice (Eds.), *Advances in educational interpreting*. Gallaudet University Press.

Kusters, A., Spotti, M., Swanwick, R., & Tapio, E. (2017). Beyond languages, beyond modalities: Transforming the study of semiotic repertoires. *International Journal of Multilingualism, 14*(3), 219–232.

Larsen, F. A., & Damen, S. (2014). Definitions of deafblindness and congenital deafblindness. *Research in Developmental Disabilities, 35*(10), 2568–2576.

Leigh, I. W., Andrews, J. F., Harris, R. L., & Ávila, T. G. (2020). *Deaf culture: Exploring deaf communities in the United States.* Plural Publishing.

Leigh, I. W., & O'Brien, C. A. (2019). Deaf identities: Exploring new frontiers. New York: Oxford University Press.

Luft, P. (n.d.). *Addressing challenges to the pool of IDEA-qualified teachers of deaf and hard-of-hearing students.* https://www.ceasd.org/wp-content/uploads/2020/03/Shortages.pdf

McCaskill, C., Lucas, C., Bayley, R., & Hill, J. (2011). *The hidden treasure of Black ASL: Its history and structure.* Gallaudet University Press.

McQuarrie, L., & Cundy, L. (2019). *The American Sign Language Phonological Awareness Test (ASL-PAT).* Sign2Read Literacy Initiatives.

Meeks, D. R. (2020). Dinner Table Syndrome: A phenomenological study of deaf individuals' experiences with inaccessible communication. *The Qualitative Report, 25*(6), 1676–1694.

Musyoka, M. M., & Adeoye, S. O. (2020). Designing an inclusive culturally competent classroom for immigrant deaf students in the United States. In K. Sprott, J. R. O'Connor Jr., & C. Msengi (Eds.), *Designing culturally competent programming for PK-20 classrooms* (pp. 180–197). IGI Global.

Neff, K. D., & Germer, C. K. (2013). A pilot study and randomized controlled trial of the Mindful Self-Compassion program. *Journal of Clinical Psychology, 69*(1), 28–44.

Oliva, G. A., Lytle, L. R., Hopper, M., & Ostrove, J. M. (2016). From social periphery to social centrality: Building social capital for deaf and hard-of-hearing students in the 21st century. In M. Marschark, V. Lampropoulou, & E. K. Skordilis (Eds.), *Diversity in deaf education* (pp. 325–354). Oxford University Press.

Ortega, L. (2020). The study of heritage language development from a bilingualism and social justice perspective. *Language Learning, 70*, 15–53.

Pichler, D. C., Reynolds, W., & Palmer, J. L. (2019). Multilingualism in signing communities. In S. Montanari & S. Quay (Eds.), *Multidisciplinary perspectives on multilingualism: The fundamentals* (Vol. 19, pp. 175–204). Walter De Gruyter.

Roeser, R., Schonert-Reichl, K. A., Jha, A., Cullen, M., Wallace, L., Wilensky, R., . . . Harrison, J. (2013). Mindfulness training and reductions in teacher stress and burnout: Results from two randomized, waitlist-control field trials. *Journal of Educational Psychology, 105*(3), 787–804.

Rosen, R. (2017). Isms, identities and intersectionality: Implications and integration. In K. Christensen (Ed.), *Educating Deaf students in a multicultural world* (pp. 57–93). DawnSignPress.

Schonert-Reichl, K. A., Oberle, E., Lawlor, M. S., Abbott, D., Thomson, K., Oberlander, T. F., & Diamond, A. (2015). Enhancing cognitive and social–emotional development through a simple-to-administer mindfulness-based school program for elementary school children: A randomized controlled trial. *Developmental Psychology, 51*(1), 52–66.

Shaw, R., & Thumann, M. (2012). Signed language academic papers. *International Journal of Interpreter Education, 4*(2), 76–88.

Simms, L., Baker, S., & Clark, M. D. (2013). The standardized Visual Communication and Sign Language Checklist for Signing Children. *Sign Language Studies, 14*(1), 101–124.

Simms, L., Rusher, M., Andrews, J. F., & Coryell, J. (2008). Apartheid in deaf education: Examining workforce diversity. *American Annals of the Deaf, 153*(4), 384–395.

Simms, L., & Thumann, H. (2007). In search of a new, linguistically and culturally sensitive paradigm in deaf education. *American Annals of the Deaf, 152*(3), 302–311.

Skyer, M. E. (2020). Invited article: The bright triad and five propositions: Toward a Vygotskian framework for deaf pedagogy and research. *American Annals of the Deaf, 164*(5), 577–591.

Slade, S., & Griffith, D. (2013). A whole child approach to student success. *KEDI Journal of Educational Policy, 10*(3), 21–35.

Swanwick, R. (2017). Translanguaging, learning and teaching in deaf education. *International Journal of Multilingualism, 14*(3), 233–249.

Valdés, G., Poza, L., & Brooks, M. D. (2015). Language acquisition in bilingual education. In W. E. Wright, S. Boun, & O. García (Eds.), *The handbook of bilingual and multilingual education* (pp. 56–74). Wiley.

Valli, C., & Lucas, C. (2000). *Linguistics of American Sign Language: An introduction*. Gallaudet University Press.

Wang, Q., & Andrews, J. F. (Eds.). (2020). *Literacy and deaf education: Toward a global understanding*. Gallaudet University Press.